Two Baths

By Julien Fannon

Foreword by Jeremy Fannon

ISBN: 979-8-218-25675-3

Printed in the United States of America

Contents

To,

My dad, who gave me the pen, showed me the way, and lent me his trust.

My mom, who loved and cried and told me to keep going.

Liam, who kept me laughing, sane, and inspired me to try again.

Matt, who soothed my soul, cradled me through it all, and pushed me forward.

Foreword,

I want to start this foreword with an admission: I can not objectively introduce this book. I have a bias that started 26 years ago on October 4th 1996. That is the day that Julien Fannon was born. That is the day I became a father for the first time. Julien Fannon is my first-born child and my bias runs deep and true.

Typically, forewords for books are written by famous, or more well-known, people as a way to introduce the author. I am a virtual unknown who has been writing a novel of my own for over a decade. A story that has been in my head for going on forty years. So why is a high school English teacher, who moonlights as a college professor, being asked to write this foreword? Does reading and teaching literature to eighteen and nineteen year-olds make me an authority on poetry? Probably not.

So, why am I writing this foreword? Because I was asked by my first-born child to write it, and there is nothing I would not do for them. Like I said, my bias runs deep and true. I also know the author about as well as anyone on this Earth, except for maybe their partner Matt. Oh, and their mother Alicia. Oh and maybe their brother Liam. I guess number four on this list is OK. It's good company.

Julien has always been a creative child. I remember when they were very young, probably two years old, dancing around our living room to Brittney Spears. I remember when they came to me as a first grader and told me that they wanted to sing in the talent show that year. My baby up on stage singing their heart out, so brave, always so brave. There I was, right up front, the proudest of fathers, admiring Julien's bravery. I have always had a front row seat to this show. There were countless school productions throughout elementary and middle school. In high school there were plays and Improv shows. In college I sat in that front row seat and watched Julien perform a one person show. The show was a very revealing look at my first-born's life. I probably learned some things that a dad did not need to know about his child. But I have never, ever regretted being in that front row. I have cherished every moment of Julien's talented life.

Julien always showed talent as an actor, but their real talent, I felt, was in their drawing and writing. This brings us to this book, and this foreword. I remember towards the end of high school, Julien came to me and we had a deep discussion about what path they would pursue in life. Would they pursue acting? Art? Writing? As a parent, I have always wanted just one thing for my kids: Happiness. I want them to be successful, whatever that means. Society typically measures success by the size of an individual's bank account. But I knew that this was not the way Julien would measure their success. I knew it would be measured by their

path of artistic expression. So I offered this advice:
"pursue your passions." It was the start of a very long
journey that has brought us all here, reading these
words.

This has been a long journey for Julien. It has not been
an easy one. To feel comfortable in their own skin for
the first time in their life. To feel like they can just be.
Without trying to fit a mold created by society, or their
Dad, or anyone else. This is a journey that submerged
and almost drowned Julien's creative spirit. But they
have surfaced from the depths of this dark place and
now the creative juices are flowing once again so
easily from their pen, and I am back in the front row. I
have missed this place up front, tears are in my eyes as
I am moved by their talent all over again. But as I have
said...

I have a bias that is decades old. It runs deep and true.

So, don't take my word for it, read this book. Go on this
journey, and see for yourself.

Jeremy

SUBMERGE

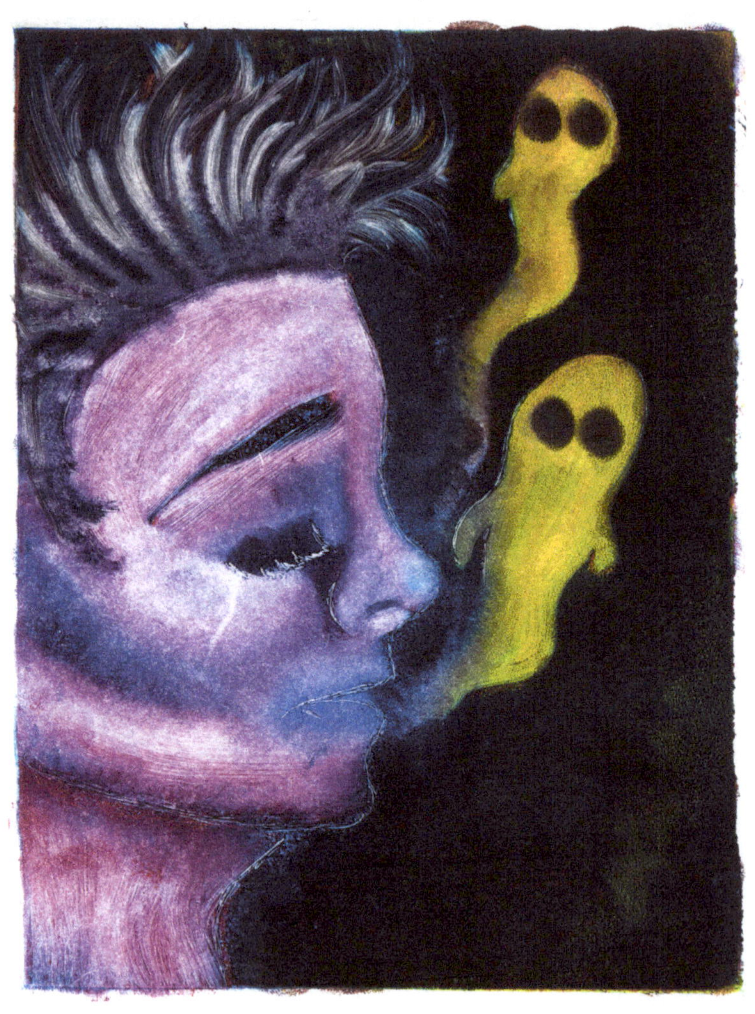

Phantom,

There is a ghost in my head and
he is without any limbs, yet
I can feel every one of his toes
sprouting cracks on the brittle
ice of my brain.
I submerge myself in boiling water
to drive him away
but we both know
that memories are not
so easily melted.

Decomposition,

I will let the flowers on my bedside
wither and wilt
until their petals fall into my hair as I slumber.
I cannot bring myself to throw them out,
to let them go and accept the loss.
somehow the more they decay
the sweeter they smell,
and the more they remind me
of you.

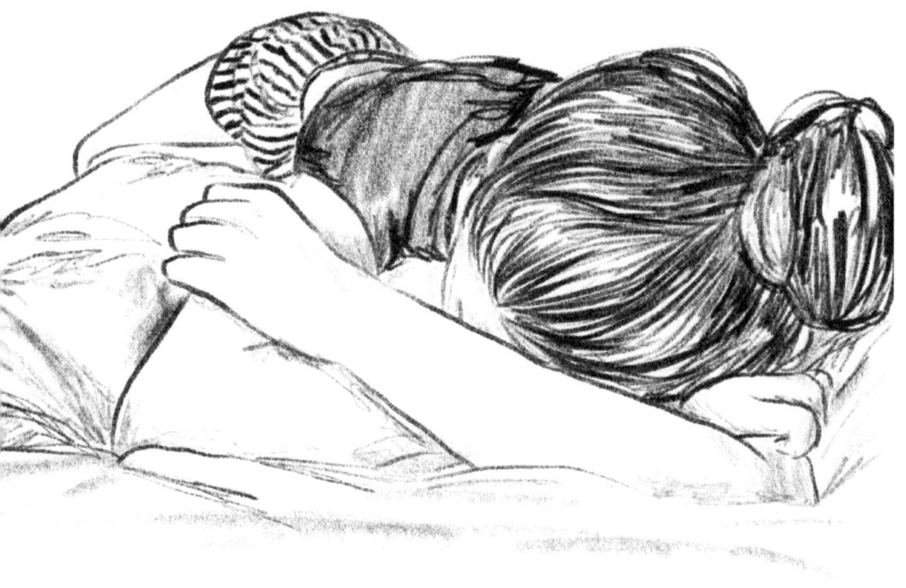

Brain surgery,

In my brain there are many things
flowers bloom in the corners of each cerebral
wrinkle
and nameless pill bugs crawl out between the
cracks
when I am feeling lonely
my memories are leaves on trees
that shrivel up and flutter away when they are
forgotten
deep down in its roots are thoughts I cannot
forget
no matter how hard I try to dig and pull them
away
from my tired mind
My brain is a cluttered foggy place
but I think the pill bugs like it that way.

Stranger,

Sometimes I find myself falling in love
with strangers.
Out on the street,
bundled up with blushing noses
from kissing the cold.
I became infatuated with the dirt caked
fingernails of the boy at the airport
and how they might have become so rough.

When I fell in love with you
I fell in love with a stranger.
And although I mused about your hands
and cold nose
and how your scarf kept you from speaking,
You left me still a stranger and
nothing more.

Precipitous,

Curious how you can
Make me feel so big and
Then small in a moment.
One breath can trickle
Down my spine and peel
Away the skin,
Exposing the delicate spines
Beneath the surface I so
Gingerly tucked away.
How precipitous of it
All to crawl into me
And tug out the
Ugly antiques from my chest
To display to your friends,
Seemingly ignorant to
How they may perceive the
Worst parts of me.
I can grow through the
Cracks in my pavement
And let the warmth
Flush my cheeks for the
First time in decades
Only to be plucked from the
Earth, roots and all.

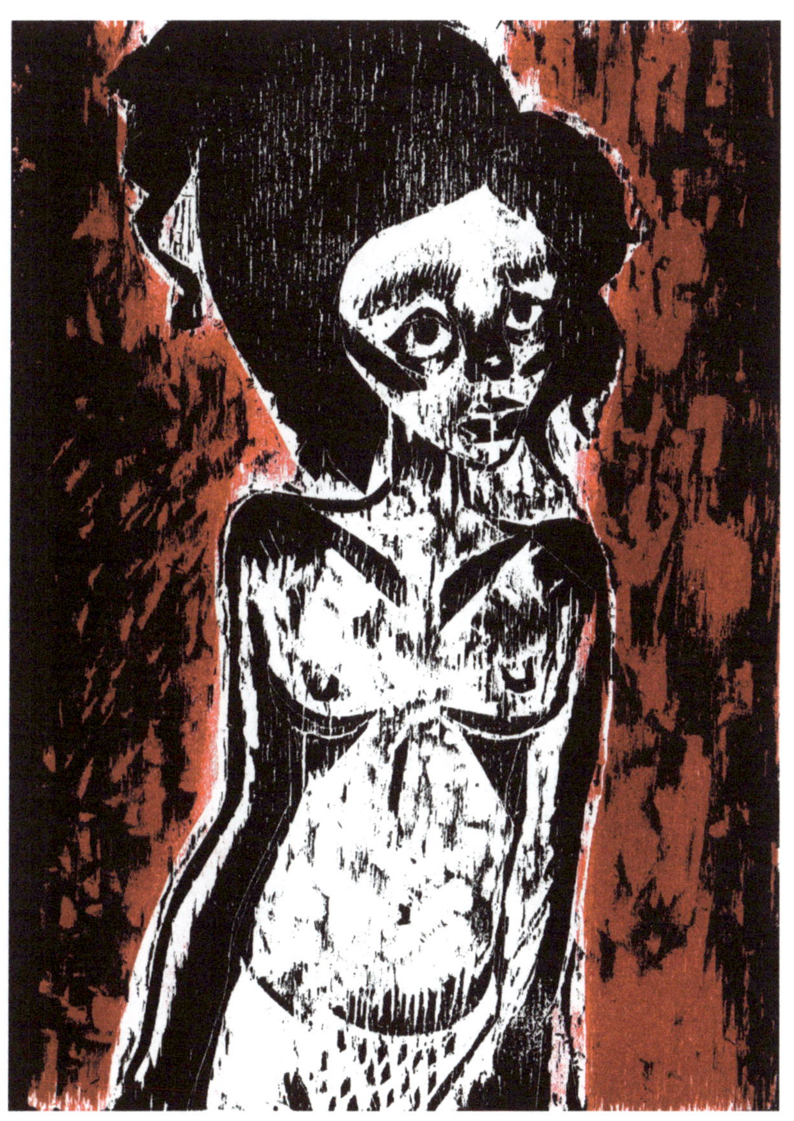

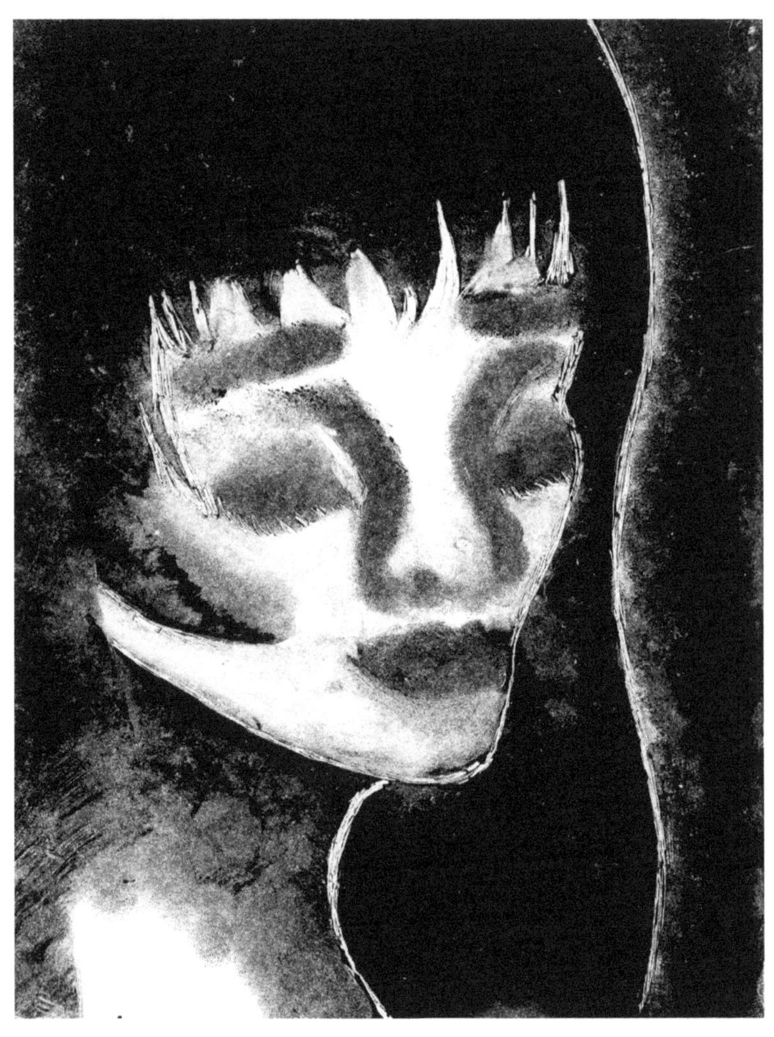

Motherhood,

Filling holes in the canvas
with hot auburns and gloomy
plums, she creates an image
of herself in acrylic.
Blue hills rolling with
jagged grass like the
lightning bolts peppered
on the soft flesh of her stomach.
The tree,
brushed starkly in tempered hues
of brown and black.
Branches swirling with each stroke
and giving birth to fireflies in the
limbs of her mind.
Covered in burls and sap,
she is her most beautiful.

Shapeshifting,

The smoke from the incense in the corner
isn't nearly enough to fog up my
cluttered mind.
Fixating on the tiny spider crawling
amongst dingy nylon and polyester,
I try to forget how fascinating you are.
It scales the scuffed drywall and
your soft voice is still echoing off
Every inch of me.

I pretend I am the spider but I
am weaving lines and lines
of prose around your neck to
keep you warm.
But I know I am
suffocating you so I pretend to be
a budding daisy in a wood so alive
and sweet.
Then I am brushing against
your toes,
the grass tinting the flesh chartreuse
And I am back again and again to
Freckled cheeks and
Belly laughs and
Palms brushing my
Blotchy knees

No matter how much I brood over
this minute insect
I cannot shake you out
Through my ears and away
Away
Away

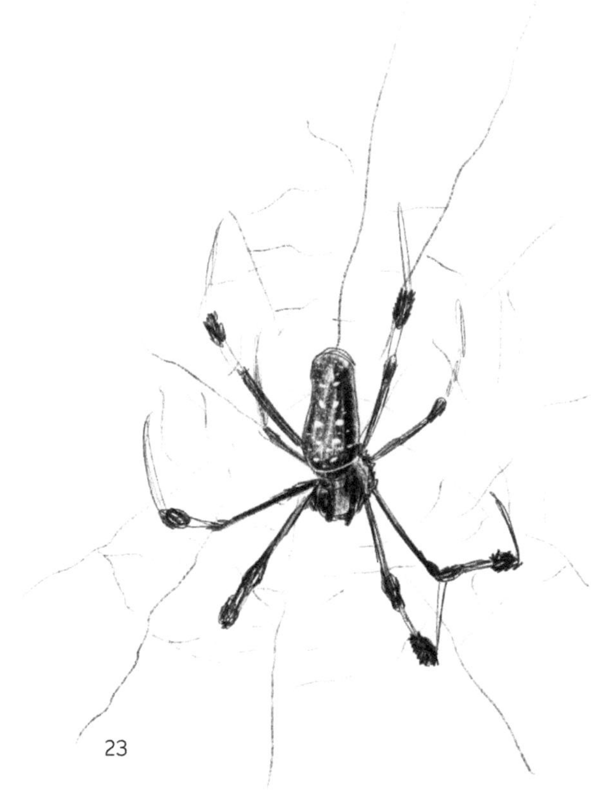

Depart,

We had a sleepover to forget that
you were wilting.
We ate ice cream and you joked
about how strange it was that
we were considered adults.
I laughed even though it scared me
that you didn't want to go out.
Like dust we swept your pain under a rug
and continued playing make-believe.
Your coughing crimson at 1am
broke the rose colored illusion.
I let you leave.
Maybe it was because I couldn't drive
or maybe it was that I was afraid you were
becoming a ghost.
I didn't realize until now
Now that I can't see me laughing without you
Now that I found a drop of blood next to your new
shoes
I would have gladly broken a thousand laws
for you.

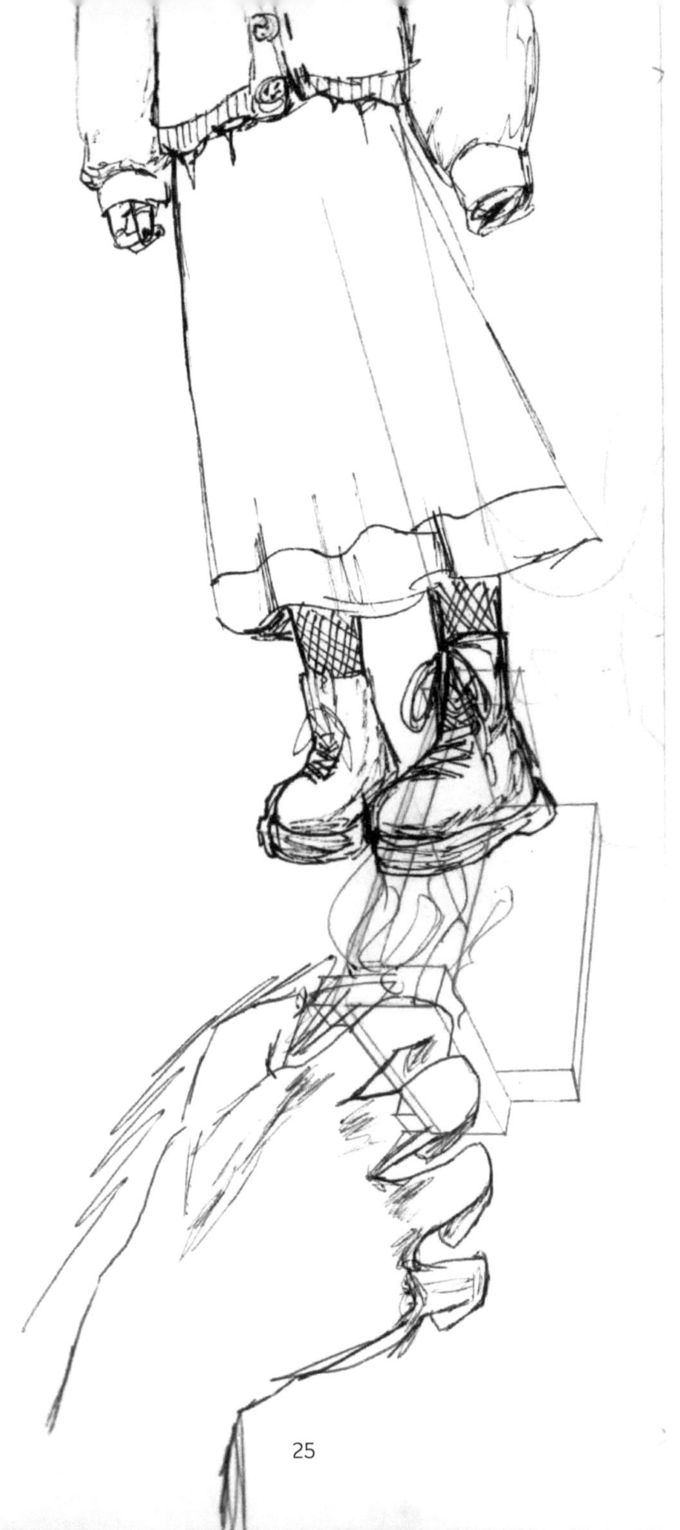

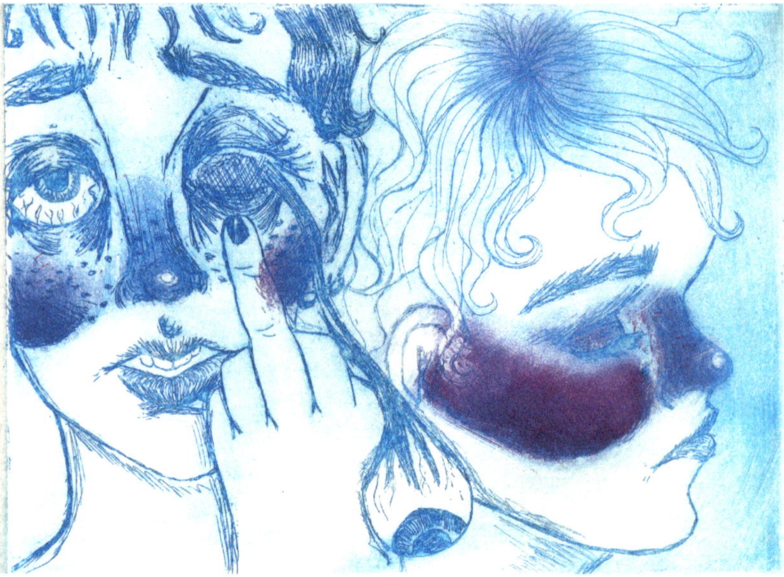

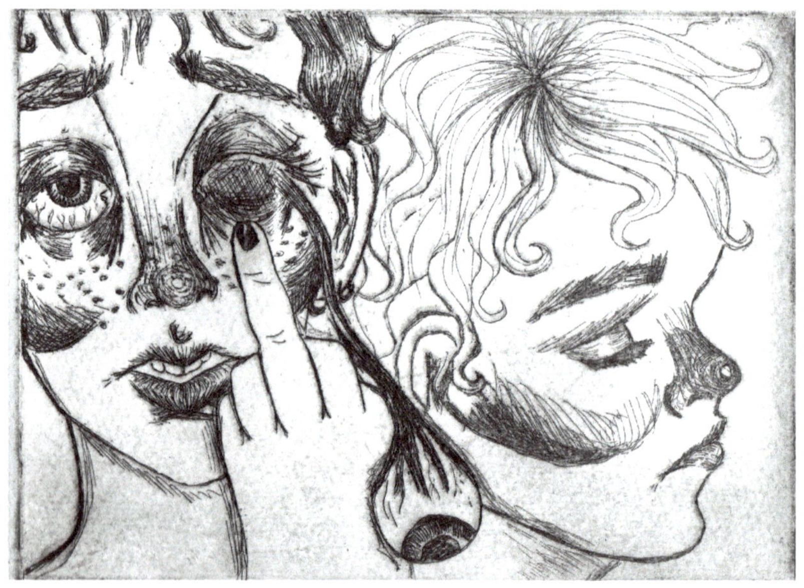

I used to write,

I don't remember crying
this much as a kid
Crawling through bramble
And serrated pebbles like
Plush velvet kissing my palms
And toes with cuts and calluses
Everyone is my friend

A look crushes me
A graze against my arm
Sends me into a crumpled sphere
Against my chalky wall
Painting my flesh with
Pinks and reds
And violet

Why am i like this
Why am i like this
Why am i like this

Remnants,

Why do I allow myself
to be like this?
To crawl back into
myself and watch
the pill bugs scatter
into the cracks
and I will try and
try and
try to fill in the
gaps with cement
and stomp the pieces
back into place of my
façade and let it
all squish between
my calloused toes
but the cooling comfort
of my feet stuck in
the most fragile parts of
me, the parts I cover up
and let rot,
they always remain
Stinking
And the same.

Mulling,

I don't know why I always
feel like this.
Why I always do this
to myself and force
crumbling limbs and
chipped fingernails
to pick up all the
pieces.
I am so tired.
I don't know if I'll
ever get married or
allow myself to feel I
could be wanted in
a realistic way.
I only see myself as
someone to be stuck with.
A trap I've set for
myself to trip over and
sink into the rotting brush
beneath me.
How could this be any
different?

Scrap paper,

Sometimes I forget that
I am more than my parts.
That crooked teeth
and straw hair
doesn't mean I'm
confined to cornfields.
I look at myself
through the mirror
I cracked when I was ten
the same way I hold
an old journal.
The nostalgic familiarity of
purple pens and
blue pens and
green pens all
running together to
tell a tale of
imperfect adolescence.
I can hear the reds
scrawling swears to
the moon and any
celestial objects I learned about
in eighth grade science
and I promise
it's thunderous.
I've been writing red

since I was twelve and
it took all the pennies
in my adventure jar
to stop myself from
rose-tinting the rest of me.

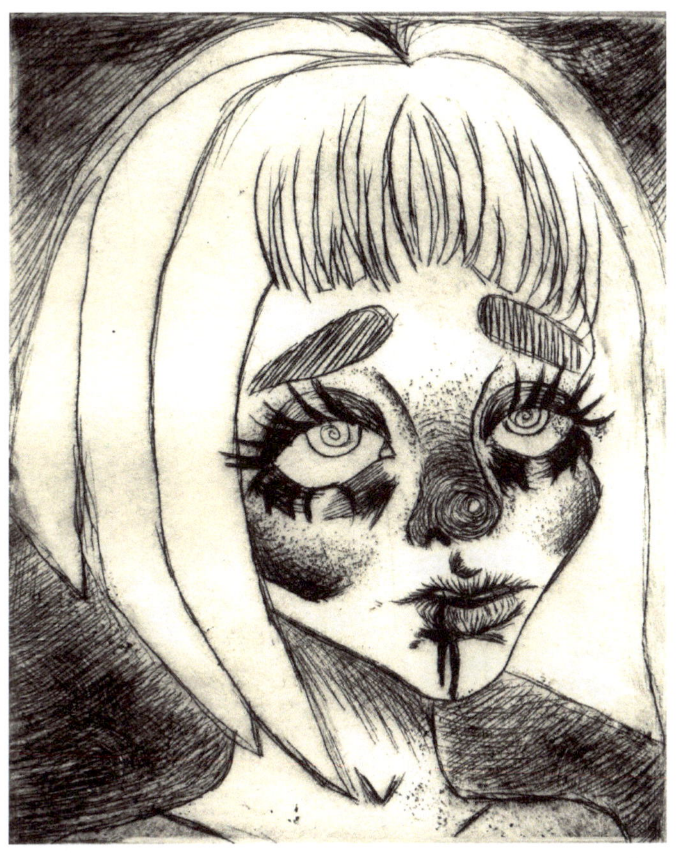

SURFACE

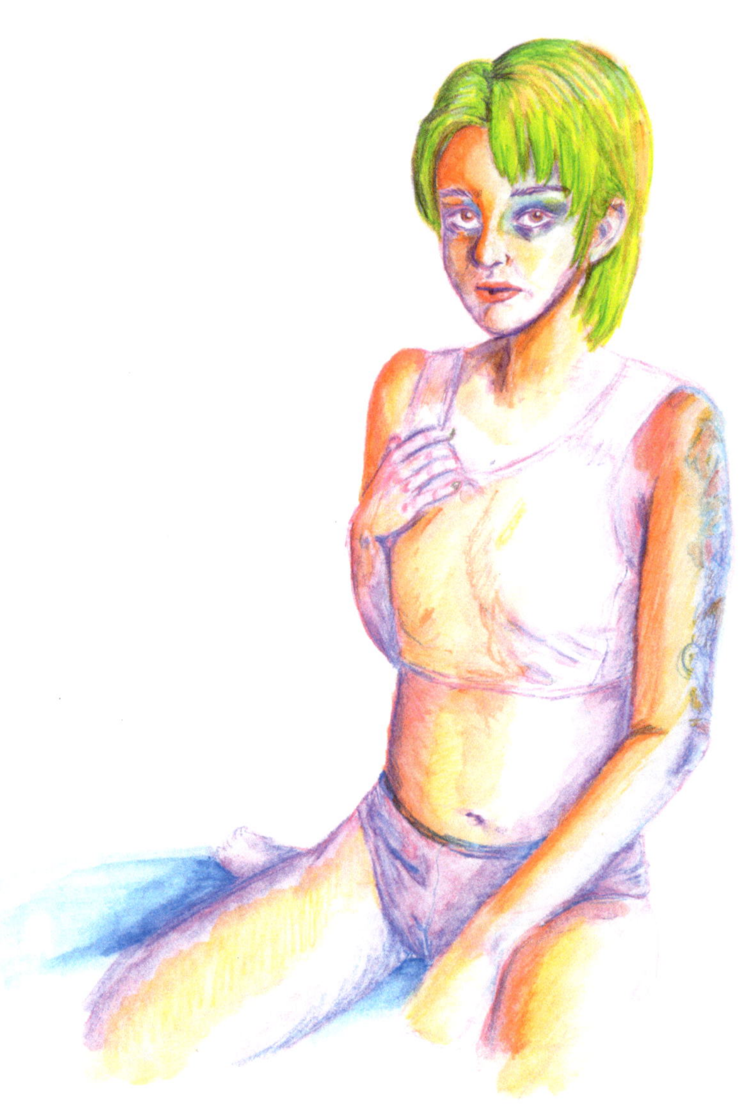

Moth boy,

Since my own smallness
I have attracted tiny things.
Earth caked pitter patters
Dancing up the driveway
Plucking daisies into
Golden twine pushed
Behind my newly pierced ears.

Calling out during a rain storm
Mud painting princess garb
As I save each slug and snail
From being whisked away in
The rapids forming in the
Sidewalk cracks.

Plump fingers leave trails
Of reds and greens as
I devour all I can about them
In borrowed books.
I could never know enough.
These little friends I made
Along the way could transform
Rapidly and without hesitation.

I know it all
Crawling and skittering

And buzzing around my frame
Yet I could not give myself permission
To do what they do
To get so big I need to curl up
And unleash something else;
Someone else.
Sputtering out excuses and
Hiding my form in bounds of
Spandex and spiderwebs
Until I am no longer her.

I have to do it

Dissolving myself
And feasting on the
Embarrassment
Until my limbs finally
Puncture and plunge
Throughout the crumbling
Sinew and I am
Gasping in breaths
Through the slime
Sputtering again but
This time the breaths
Come in easy
Unbound and sewn back
Up by my own golden twine
And daisy chains.

Wiping away the grime
With gentle hands and
Soothing hymns
I am back.

Silken wings brushing by
And lifting my new form
Back back back
Into the sun again.

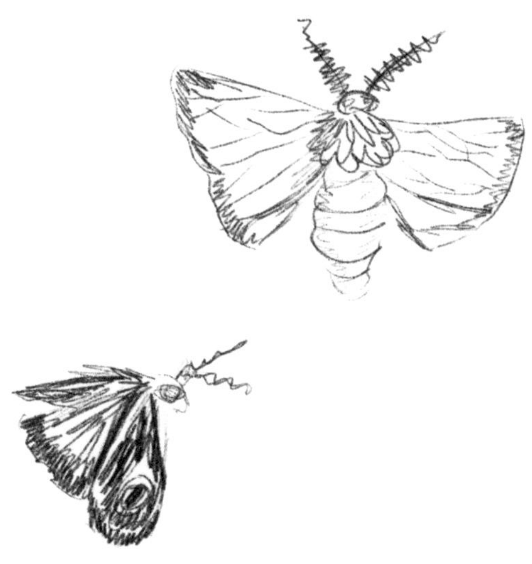

Two Baths,

Pouring kettle brewed
Warmth over me
My skin recalls
The moments my mother
Did the same.

Plastic cups filled
With suds she gingerly
Palms my brow,
Protecting my face from
The stinging remnants of the day
Washing over me.
She hums soft tunes and
Spoons me into her lap
Drifting me into calm.

Today I spend extra care to
Caress the raised scar
Jutting across my breast,
Cutting me into two and
Forgiving me for forgetting
Myself for so long.
I hum my mothers songs
Out of key but
Still feel as small as I
Did decades before.

I am learning to mother myself
Despite it all,
Changing and growing
Like a child
Holed up inside of me
And bursting out with each
Searing drop.

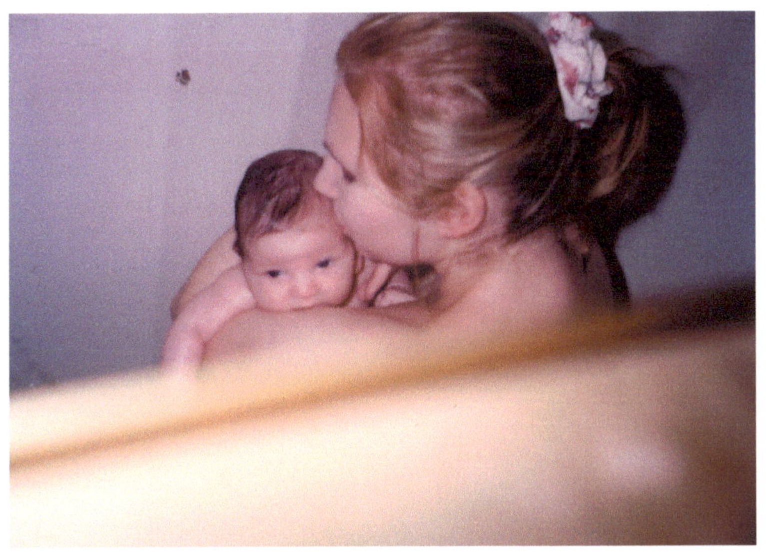

26,

I am 26
But I am still a child.
I collect bottle caps
Along the river
Squishing my toes
Deeper and deeper
Into sludge
And packing up
Pebbles and sand dollars
Into my lunch box,
My thumb sized treasures
Clinging against the tin
Like soft symphonies.

I am 26
But I am an old old man.
Kissing my wife on her cheeks
And sorting my yarn
Into color coded candies
On my desk side
Weathered fingers tapping
Plastic needles into
Rainbows of warmth and comfort
Before promptly settling into bed
When the last rays slip
Below the window pane.

I am 26
And I am split into
Shattered facets of stone and
Glass and crystal
Sending tinted specs of
Sun across your
Sap smeared eyes.
You cup me back together
And we sink into the earth again.

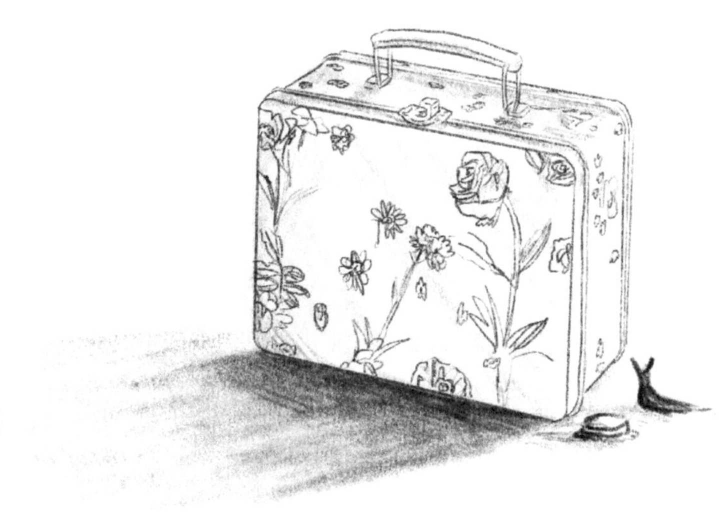

Helen,

What would she say about me?
The sticky handed child
That lovingly peppered
Hand crafted ornaments
On her Christmas tree
Each season in her
Big white house far away?

She guided my hands
Along tinkering keys
Of the dusty grand piano
In the corner.
It smells of warm
Tobacco and wool
As I play Heart and Soul
Over and Over again
To impress her and him—
Wherever he may be.

What would she think
Of me now,
Sweaty and walking
By the old big white house
Not so far away now?
Is she with him,
Humming Heart and Soul

And brushing tobacco off
The arms of his coat?

I hope she can see
The me I am now,
Even stickier than before
In this heat,
Love aching in my chest
And tapping by
Her house each day.

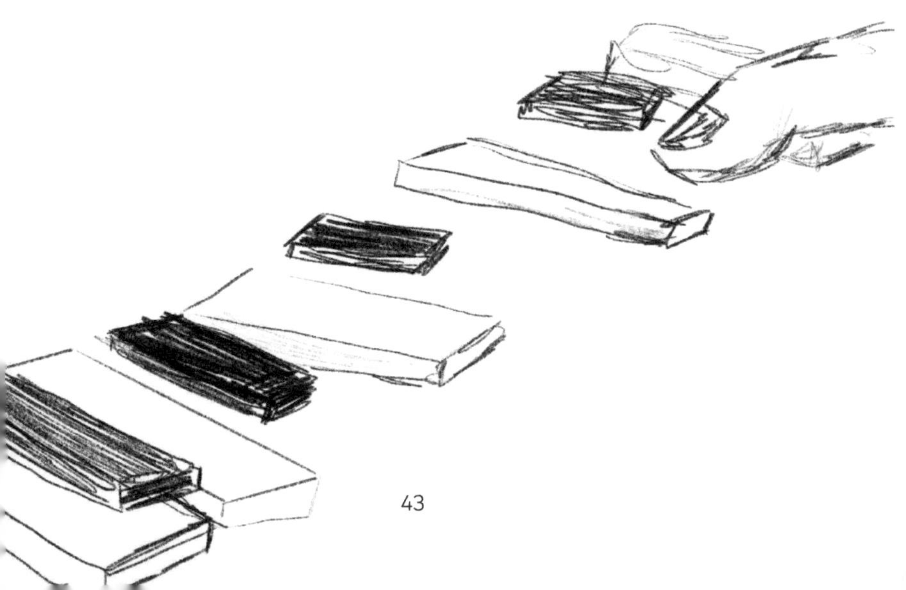

How do I write about the Writer?

He does not create
In traditional ways,
But has mastered
Holding space for others
Like he brushed
Heavy hands along the joints
Of an overwhelmed child
To soothe his fears of
The world.

He heals with action
And dives in deeply,
Learning and loving
All that he can quietly.
He answers with soft
Hymns just when you
Need it,
Crushing doubts with
A hand firmly on your shoulder,
Even if it is him
Who shoulders the rest.

I've known this,
Even when I've fought
With doors slamming and
Shoes tossed against the wall.

Still he patches me up,
Adjusts his words,
Learns again and again,
And walks through the
Door again to embrace
Another me.

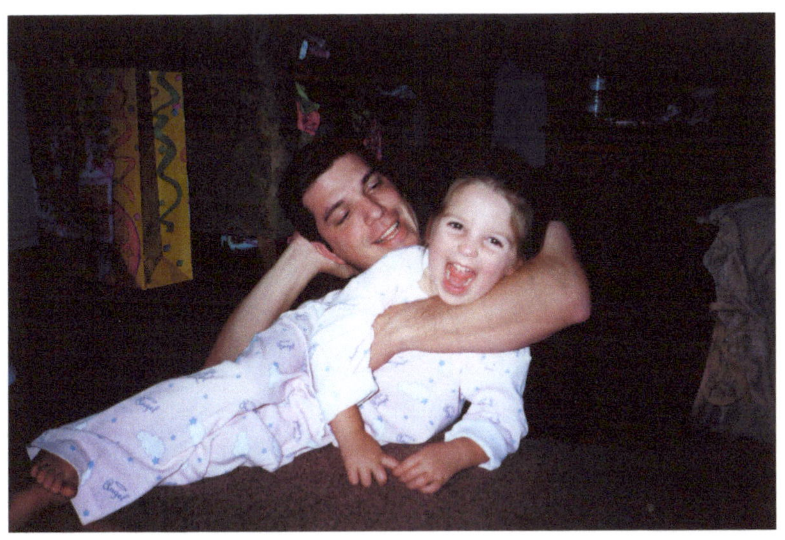

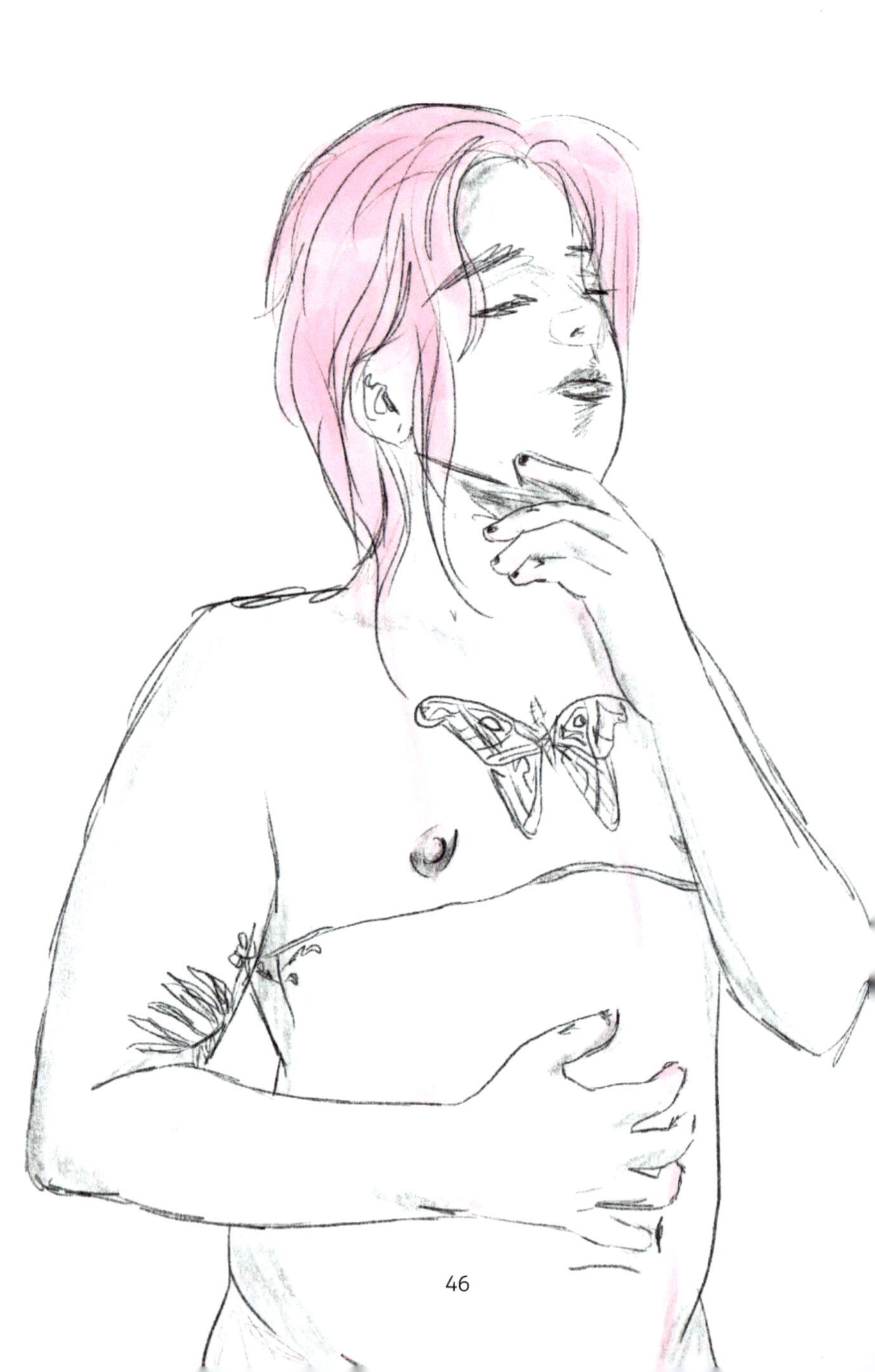

Pools of Pink,

The lady at the mall
Well intentioned
Brushes me with
Tales of how her
Younger self would be
Just like me.

I think of my crooked
Spine and soft
Stomach dripping with
Pinks and blues
In my too-hot
Too often
Teal bath house;
How I don't know when
I'd ever stop taking these
Little moments for just me.
Even hunch backed
And caked with
70 years of being
Finally this body
Could I ever be that
Lady in the mall
Wishing I allowed
Myself the simple pleasure
Of being colorful and
Alive.

Cut,

I remember you
Hiding behind the
Golden thread,
Afraid to snip even
An inch.
A safety blanket
Cloaking me in girlhood
While I buried myself deeper.

Finding the words for
The clambering in my chest
Terrified me to no end.
The smattering of phrases
Clattering around my being
Finally realized and
Oozing out the cracks.

Cutting it away
Felt like a treat
Like I'd been craving
The weight off my shoulders
The gentle tapping of the
Scissors against my nape
Unspooling the fibers
I'd woven around myself

Despite the blistering air,

I am back to growing again.
Spinning the threads into
Candy floss that brushes my
Freckled collar and weaving
That little me back in.

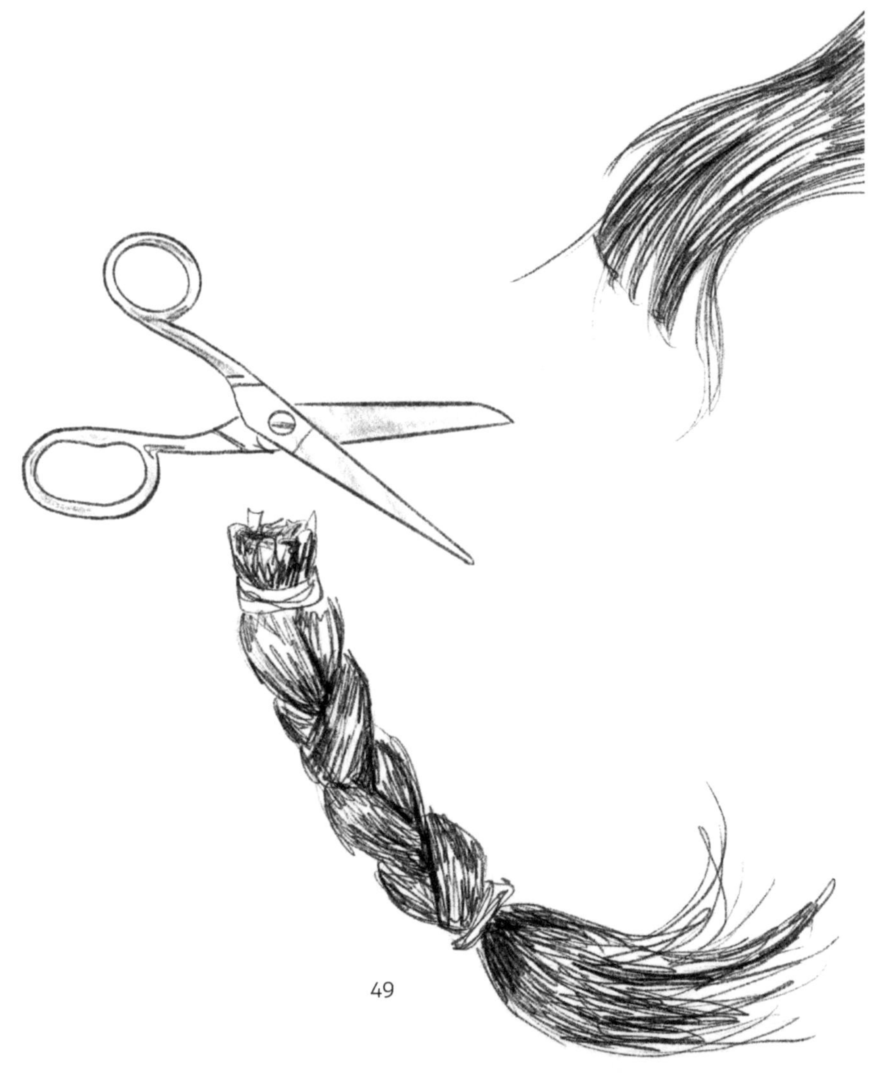

49

Dig me out,

I wonder how long
I've buried myself.

Instead I've been plucked
From pot to pot
Never knowing
All I needed was
more space to
sink into the ground.
Spread my roots and learn
To shear away the parts
That owned me for so long.

How do you forget yourself so easily?
I long for the moments
I would throw anything out
Into the world,
Kicking and screaming
And begging for nothing
From anyone.

When did I get scared to
Put on the dress?
Shame clawed
Into me and discarded me into
The box I so desperately

longed to obliterate.

I can be sweet and
Raise an octave
And blow kisses
And smear the lipstick
And laugh too loud.

I can be all and nothing at once
And both at the same time
And none
And none
And none
At all.

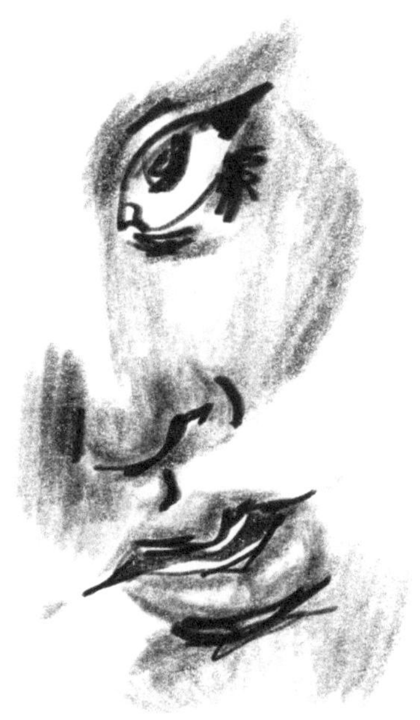

Drag,

Why do they hate us so much?
I am just
Sitting and trying to
Gather the courage
To hold up the pieces
I finally put together
I've kept locked
In the cash box
Under my bed
Buried in the back
Next to my sharpied
Barbie dolls.

I jumped through
Flaming hoops
Singing the hair off my
Throbbing skull
And groveling on the floor
Begging for one
Drop of decency.
Spent months
Relearning and
Shedding the doubt
Like a second skin
That tucked me in and away
For two decades

Protecting me until I could
Crack open and
Spill out
And out
The cracks.

I am quietly filling
In the gaps with
Who I've wanted to be
For so long until
There are so many tiny
Shards in me that I
Overflow
And soil the fun and
Yell and yell
And beg
Please
Just this once
Leave us the fuck alone.
Just this once.

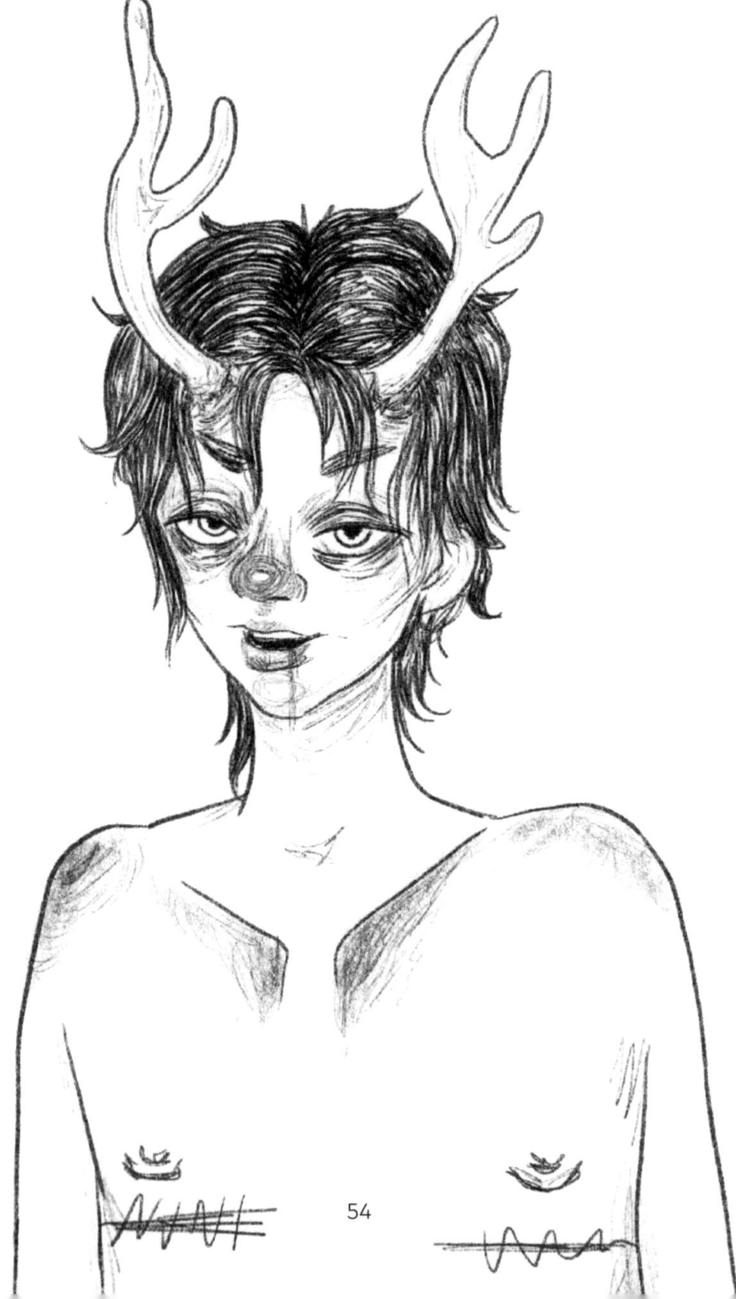

Kill me,

My eyes flutter
Open and the first
Thing I see along
With the threads of light
Beaming through the fog
Is how much they want us dead.

I have wanted this
For myself before
And I know that tapping
Up my spine until it
Presses on the fibers of
My skull and tells me to
Leave in five million ways.

Today I am terrified
And rash and loud
And mean about it all.
For the first time in my life
So it seems
I want to live.
I crave the sun on my back
And chest turning too pink
Along the cracks.

All I've done is finally

Cradle myself tenderly
Watering the seeds
Of this real,
Unequivocal me.
We are finally kind to ourselves
And you are so scared
So horrified that there
Could possibly be a way
To be alive that isn't
Cut and dry
Black and white
Pink and Blue.

I know you expect
Us to crumble and
Beg for you to change your
Cement minds
But instead I will kick
And scream and
Spit in your boring
Fucking face
And see if you can
Try to drag me from this
Earth.
I will never
Ever
Leave.

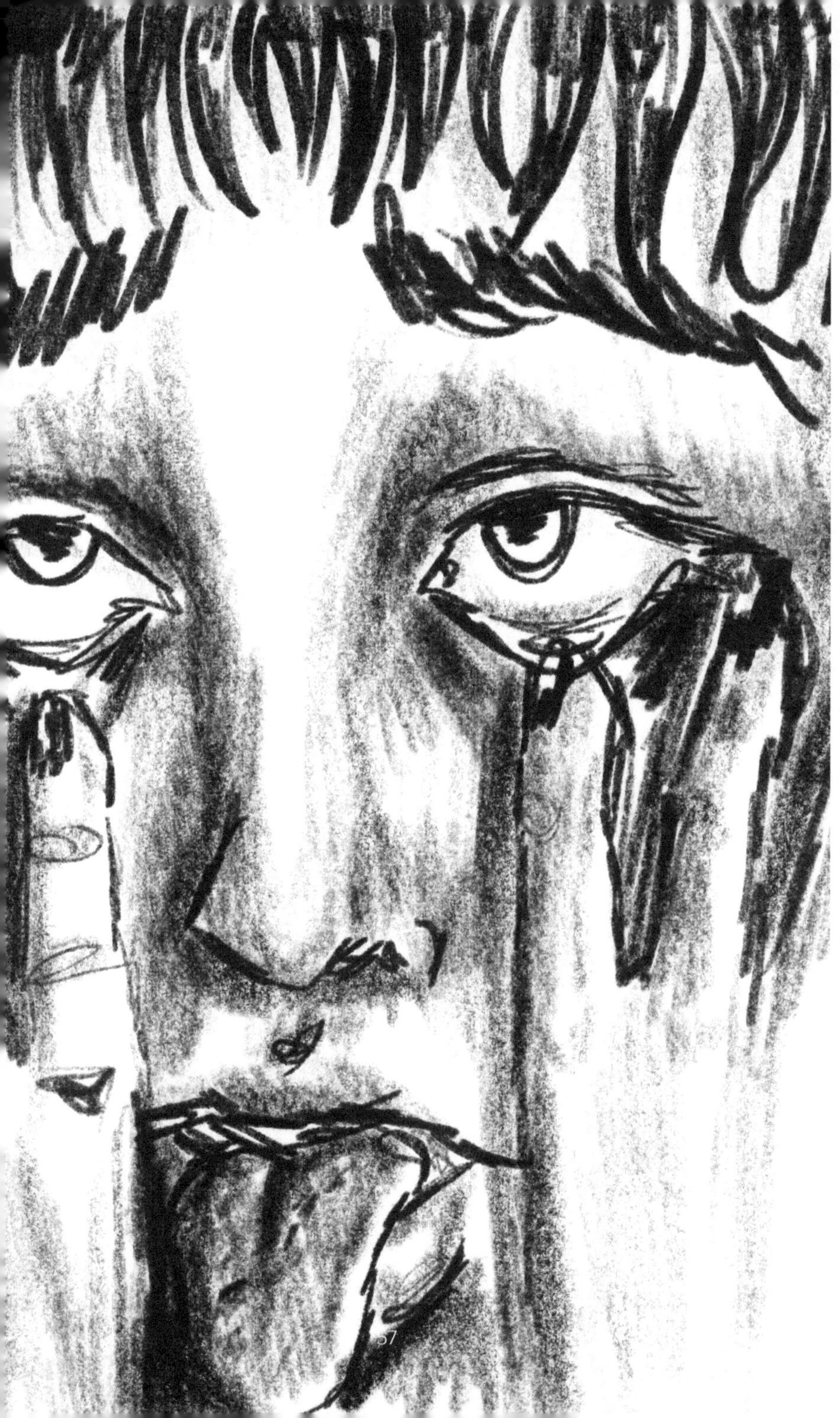

Shield,

Feral
Cascading and crawling
Through silken earth
And razor blade brush
I am free

Take my toes
One by one
And I will not change

Whatever I am
Whoever I am
It's fine
And long overdue

Pass the bills
Left and right
I will protect the posterity
More than you ever could,
Trust dripping from my lips
Like a song
And pasting together
Their wounds with craft glue
And papier-mâché.

You cannot decide
The fears deep
Within their gut
Growing with each
Spark of love you snuff out.

I have taken each step
Through broken glass
Slicing through me until
I am a paper doll
Reforming again and again.
I grasp the hand of those
Cast away from you,
Your silken gowns and sickly
Perfume like armor that penned the
Way to be a real woman.

Skewer me with your
Proverbs and passing remarks
You will never kill me
You can never silence us
Death comes to your kin from
You and you alone.

She she she,

They will never be as tender
To cup me,
A tiny bud,
In her bruised arms
Sewing me up and
Sowing the seeds
In me that I could not.

She does not know
Tenderness from anyone
Else yet
She offers me old rags
That encompass me and
Swallow me whole
But let the good parts
Poke out into the surface at last.

She takes me by the hand
And shows me card tricks
And old tales of hiding
And how to fill my glass
Until it overflows

She nods her head and
Cuts her own bangs
And tells me yes yes

You're you now
And I am me
And I will not let go.
She lets me put on her lipstick
Even if I go outside the lines
And she lets me laugh and laugh
With her friends.

They will never be as tender
No they could never.

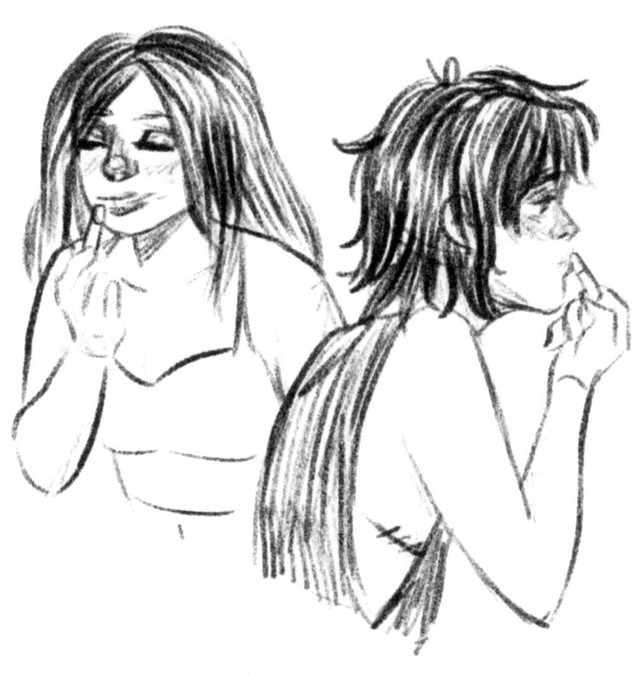

Matrimony,

I am so exhausted
From being nice
The pit in my stomach
Grows so large
I wish you'd choke on it.

The pleasantries are insufferable
Vomiting out through
Turned up lips
I cranked alive like
The windows of my first car

I'd love to rip out the seams,
Sputtering and snapped
Under the pressure.

I can never be a diamond
For you and
I don't want to be.

I am not your baby doll,
God given to your son
Like John or Isiah
Ready to be tied up in
Silk and smiling.

But I am soft
And supple with soothing
hymns to heal
The tiny fractures
Aching along his spine

He reaches into
The heavens with
Nothing now,
And still I am his apostle
Ever growing with him
As he falls and
Crawls back into the clouds.

At Last,

Weary watching winds
Creak through the
Cyclical window panes of
The home I finally found
With you.

Palms plush against
Rods and stitches
Brushing against
Stocking feet
Tucked into the rug to
Avoid the grime yet to
Be brushed blissfully away

I am happy again.
For once breathing
Craft store cinnamon
Penniless and plentiful all
At once,
I feel I can leap out
Into the shimmering streets
Pebbles digging into my fleshy
Heels greyed by linoleum and
Nothing can hurt me.
Not this time.

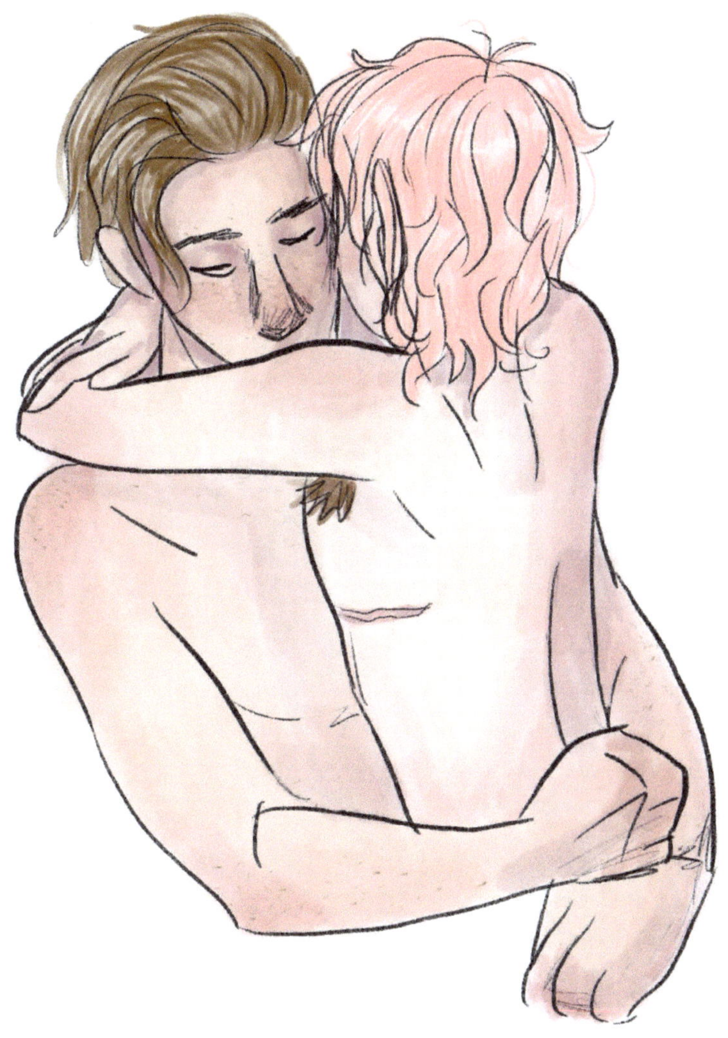

I am so lucky to be able to share these little parts of me with you. When I wrote the first half of poems in this book, I only remember feeling scared. Maybe that's not quite the right word— but there was something so deep within me that held me down under the water for so long. I thought everyone felt like me— drowned and unreal in their skin. It took so much digging to finally hit solid ground again, and drain away all this doubt.

I don't think I ever expected to feel completely right in the end, but I definitely never thought I could be so angry still. People will never understand how beautiful it is to be trans; to take the pieces and make them fit together again. To be held by those who went through hell to make things easier for you. Transness is beautiful, and magic, and will never go away.

These are the parts that are most beautiful about me, dear reader. I hope that this peak into me has helped to shift your perspective towards love, or maybe solidify it more. Everyone on this earth is deserving of the love I received during my most formative years. If you are unable to sit in a comfortable place now, please know I will love you loudly and infinitely. This space is for all of us — and especially you.

Thank you again for reading my book, and for allowing me to spend this time with you.

Trans love is revolutionary.

Always,

Julien